Keep It Clean

Energy Clearing and
Aura Illumination
Techniques for
Empaths

Keep It Clean

Energy Clearing and Aura Illumination Techniques for Empaths

Mountain Flower

 Pueblo Press

4

Keep It Clean

By Mountain Fower

Copyright © 2024 by Mountain Flower

Front cover photo:

Interior images from Pixabay, Mountain Flower, Greig OB Session, and Jason Kohl

Published by:
Pueblo Press
677 Cash Street, Croydon, NH 03773

Interior Design by Itancan Wasaka, Croatan Press

Requests for permission from:
Global Wisdom
860-303-8772
ISBN: 978-1-957878-01-0

Other Books By Mountain Flower / Leslie Karen Hammond:

Tap Your Source

Women Rising: How To Go From Uncomfortable To Unstoppable

Keep It Real; Why Were Afraid To Speak Up and What To Do About It

Holding Space: How To Help Women Feel Safe

Conversational Intelligence: Understanding Your Style To Help Others Feel Heard

Find us on social media:

Healing Through Your Story

Healing Through Your Story

medicinewoman_mountainflower

Leslie Mountain Flower Hammond

Dedication

This book is dedicated to every conscious lightworker and those in the process of awakening to their gifts. I feel you.

If it weren't for being challenged in some area of life and mustering the courage to dream and take action, you might never dive into the required healing work that supports evolving and holding your highest vibration possible.

Thousands are waking by the minute without support. Wherever you are on the journey, I am holding space for your energetic and spiritual growth as a portal for finding your next phase of grounded expansion and heart-centric service. You have so much to offer humanity. May you find support in these pages and feel my love as you explore cleansing and illumination.

Contents

Section 3 Illumination Exercises

12

Acknowledgments

A special thanks to my soul sister, Denise, who suggested I ground myself. She could feel my energetic scatteredness through the phone line and knew it wasn't my norm. As a person who is known for being grounded, I was thankful for her statement; it was enough to break up the fog where I'd gotten lost. Seeing the pattern I was stuck in would reveal profound lessons; what has transpired since is remarkable.

In the last few weeks, you'd think I've made grounding an Olympic sport! In training, my feet are on the ground as soon as my coffee is poured.

With profound thanks for having my back, I appreciate your wisdom and guidance!

Preface

Showing up physically, energetically, and emotionally to facilitate workshops or healing sessions for my clients has always come easy. Regardless of what I've been processing, keeping commitments to serve has transformed putting my drama aside for the highest good into a plethora of teaching moments.

Since asking Spirit to "bring it on" in a ceremony before the eclipse in the spring of 2024, my connection to Spirit, willingness to pivot, and downloads on what's next have increased significantly. However, so have my healing processes.

Through the darkest moments of panic and anxiety, I had forgotten much of what was on these pages. Trapped in fatigue and feeling overwhelmed, fear rose to the surface, clouding my focus and undermining productivity. Conscious of the vibration I infuse in everything I do, working was out of the question. Fortunately, this malaise lasted only a few days. What got me through was grounding and a return to my morning spiritual practices. I began some simple illumination exercises, and within days, each session revealed another depth or layer of light to add to what I already felt was a meaningful and complete protocol. Now, I can appreciate waking up early because it allows more time for me to connect, brighten my light, and step more fully into what's next. My intent is for you to experience a glowing start to each day and feel energetically protected, aligned, and inspired.

Introduction

This publication is intended to empower anyone with a pure heart and intention to start or take any self-care or healing practice to the next phase.

The enclosed exercises anyone can perform. Complete instructions are provided for everything from preparing your space to grounding afterward. Readers are encouraged to read section one for the foundational principles. Additionally, the first three chapters of section two are instrumental in getting the most from these protocols.

Your mission is to shine as brightly as possible and live in the highest vibration you can. These pages will help you get there and stay there. Chances are, as a heart-centered person, you've been giving most of your life; now, it's time to fill your cup and feel energetically whole and complete.

Medical Disclaimer: This book provides information on spiritual and alternative healing practices for educational purposes only. The content is not intended to be a substitute for professional medical advice, diagnosis, or treatment. Always seek the advice of your physician or other qualified health provider with any questions you may have regarding a medical condition. Never disregard professional medical advice or delay in seeking it because of something you have read in this book.

The spiritual practices described herein are not intended to diagnose, treat, cure, or prevent any disease. The author and publisher are not responsible for any adverse effects or consequences resulting from the use of any suggestions, preparations, or procedures described in this book. If you are pregnant, nursing, taking medication, or have a medical condition, consult your healthcare provider before using any of the practices outlined in this work.

Readers are advised to use their own judgment and consult appropriate professionals regarding their individual health needs. The information presented here should not be interpreted as medical recommendations for individual treatment plans.

By reading and implementing any of the practices in this book, you agree to take full responsibility for your health and well-being.

To facilitate assimilating the most useful information from this book, there is a section at the end for listing your biggest takeaways from each chapter.

"Trusting your intuition invites every experience to be spiritual and every idea to be a download. There is no right or wrong, only experimentation and skill-building."

                                   - *Mountain Flower*

Chapter 1

Imagination Versus Downloads

In a recent workshop to support people on their intuitive journey, I asked: "Is there a difference between a download from Spirit/your higher power and your imagination?" I've learned to trust that what comes to me through a divine whisper is a download. Once referred to it as imagination, I realized there might not be a difference. When an idea in a previously unknown realm arises, how could it be from anything other than the Divine?

Throughout this book's clearing and illumination exercises, you can expect to expand your perception of what comes into your awareness. Calling a hunch a download or an intuitive nudge is empowering. It reminds you that Spirit is always there to provide support. You'll feel more connected, alive, and guided when tapped in.

There may be a cosmic library that trickles information to you as you're ready. Who or what regulates it? Our higher power, the ancestors? Does it matter? When you deepen your capacity to sense the guidance you receive, magical things happen at an accelerated rate. I promise!

While facilitating ceremonies within sacred space, people feel the presence of their ancestors. They feel held by their higher power and loved ones who have crossed the rainbow bridge. Sometimes, experiences are so vivid that people are surprised because they never considered the possibility of connecting in such ways. Some examples of the sensations people experience are:

- Feeling breath on their cheek
- Hearing music or voices
- Seeing their guides
- Feeling the presence of loved ones
- Full body sensations

Setting your intention supports the experience you want to have. Focus on what you want instead of declaring what you do want. Keep the language positive and filled with high vibration. With an open heart and spirit, let your higher power know you're ready to experience something exceptional. Spirit always delivers.

Consider starting a new journal to note your whispers from a higher power. However often you choose to review your notes, you'll be delightfully surprised at how much progress you've made.

A quick tip to help you avoid the "one more thing" syndrome: make your notes with bullet points instead of writing paragraphs if it'll inspire continuity; sometimes, journaling can sink to the bottom of our to-do lists when we're tired.

What's the biggest takeaway from this chapter?

_____

_____

"Enlightenment is a destructive process. It has nothing to do with becoming better or being happier. Enlightenment is the crumbling away of untruth. It's seeing through the façade of pretense. It's the complete eradication of everything we imagined to be true."

– Adyashanti

Chapter 2

Trust and Truth

S taying open is necessary to support success in any realm. Your bandwidth to access broader possibilities narrows when you remain attached to previous experience.

The following exercise invites you to consider what you take as truth without question and where resistance to new concepts may be hiding. Suppose your upbringing was rooted in religion or lacking any spiritual influence. In that case, underlying doubt may cloud the possibilities of what you prefer to be true.

What five things do you trust to be true without giving them a second thought?

1. _____

2. _____

3. _____

4. _____

5. _____

Who or what continues to support each truth?

Truth1:

_____

Truth 2:

_____

Truth 3:

_____   _____

Truth 4:

_____

Truth 5:

_____

Who or what is the origination of each truth?

Truth 1:

_____

Truth 2:

_____

Truth 3:

_____

Truth 4:

_____

Truth 5:

_____

Which, if any, of these truths are you open to exploring from a spiritual or energetic perspective?

Truth 1:

_____

Truth 2:

_____

Truth 3:

_____

Truth 4:

_____

Truth 5:

_____

Of the truths you're open to exploring, which heart-centric ones are a priority? What possibilities might be ahead of you as a result?

I want _____
to be true.

The possibility ahead by being more open might be:

_____

I want _____
to be true.

The possibility ahead by being more open might be:

_____

I want _____
to be true.

The possibility ahead by being more open might be:

_____

I want _____
to be true.

The possibility ahead by being more open
might be:

_____

Expanding one's understanding of foundational
principles or values is a courageous exploration
of possibility beyond the default programming
of right and wrong. You can digest the
perspectives of masters or gurus; however,
whatever resonates must align for you. It may
take integration over an indeterminate amount
of time to realize how the new information fits
your life and creates meaning. Expect a period
of knowing where articulating what you feel is
elusive. If you have a mentor or confidant who
can listen objectively, that would be fantastic.
Otherwise, be selective about who you share
the new understanding with.

We offer spiritual mentorship to help heart-
centered people like you as you explore new

possibilities in life once your eyes open to living more connected to the sacred and how the new self integrates into relationships, careers, and public service. If you're interested, let's have a conversation and discuss how we can be of service. Schedule a 30-minute call at https://calendly.com/mtflower/connection-call

What's the biggest takeaway from this chapter?

_____

_____

"It is the Higher Power which does everything, and the man is only a tool. If he accepts that position, he is free from troubles; otherwise, he courts them."

– Ramana Maharshi

Chapter 3

Working with Your Higher Power

Building trust with your higher power is more than a one-and-done relationship; it's an ongoing relationship, as in any other, and it requires time to deepen. You'll get more comfortable. In that comfort, you'll find taking more expansive risks for the highest good easier because the guidance you get feels trustworthy.

There's also the factor of sacred reciprocity. When you ask for help and get it, it is respectful to convey your acknowledgment, gracious reception, and appreciation. The more you practice the reciprocity, the more help you get. For those new to working with spiritual or animal guides, please trust your requests are heard. Please trust what you sense when an image, a color, or a sound comes into your awareness. Guides come in many ways. As you build your relationship, you'll recognize who is who and know them more deeply.

Pay attention to how you feel when energy comes through. My guides always come for the highest good. If you sense anything less than supportive, loving energy, immediately surround yourself with light while declaring yourself powerful and protected.

Part of opening sacred space is creating a healthy, supportive, safe container to explore.

Burn a candle or wear jewelry that empowers you if you want more support.

If you've been working with any guides, list them and what they represent here:

Guide 1 _____

Representation_____

_____

Guide 2 _____

Representation_____

_____

Guide 3 _____

Representation_____

_____

Guide 4 _____

Representation_____

_____

Guide 5 _____

Representation_____

_____

If you're still learning what any of your guides represent, leave the representation lines blank and trust the information will come to you in divine time.

If there are any specific guides you'd like to begin working with, list them here:

1. _____

2. _____

3. _____

4. _____

5. _____

A fun check-in with the guides you've been working with might be to ask them if there is another characteristic they'd like to represent for you or if they are content with how they currently serve. I imagine our guides are similar to people; just because they are good at something doesn't guarantee that what they're doing is where they have the most fun.

If there are traits or characteristics you want a guide to support you in developing, list them here. You can also list the traits alone, trusting that the appropriate guide will come forth to assist you in due time. Place your orders with Spirit often and detach from the outcome.

Trait:

_____

Guide:

_____

Trait:

_____

Guide:

_____

Trait:

_____

Guide:

_____

Trait:

_____

Guide:

_____

Trait:

_____

Guide:

_____

Here's to playing in the realms of expansive possibility with divine support beyond anything you've ever imagined!

What's the biggest takeaway from this chapter?

_____
_____

"To seek the highest good is to live well."

- Saint Augustine

Chapter 4

Highest Good

To trust that anything is in the highest good is easy when things are flowing smoothly and going your way. However, when something difficult arises, such a simple statement challenges you to remember the vibrational definition.

Sometimes, the "highest good" is a healing crisis. For example, when one stops engaging in addictive behavior, the body begins a cleansing and healing process. When a person can see the cleansing as a spiritual experience, it makes the process much easier and often deeply reflective. Even stubbing a toe, spilling a coffee, or getting stuck in traffic can slow you down just enough to keep you safe.

I've had injuries that opened my eyes to thought patterns or attitudes that ran their course. Still, I was so insistent on hanging on that I needed help changing my mind. The injury was the only way to slow me down long enough to see clearly. Yes, it was bear, and I went down fighting, but the insights were extraordinary and sent me on a more aligned trajectory.

Is there anything that comes to mind for you that, when looked at from a spiritual perspective, might take on a new, more profound meaning? I encourage you to do this weekly, monthly, or quarterly exercise to realize how far you've come. The more frequently you adopt a spiritual perspective on life, the quicker it becomes second nature.

Event 1:

_____

_____

_____

Previous meaning:

_____

_____

_____

More expansive, spiritual meaning:

_____

_____

_____

Event 2:

_____

_____

_____

Previous meaning:

_____

_____

_____

More expansive, spiritual meaning:

_____

_____

_____

Event 3:

_____

_____

_____

Previous meaning:

_____

_____

_____

More expansive, spiritual meaning:

_____

_____

_____

Event 4:

_____

_____

_____

Previous meaning:

_____

_____

_____

More expansive, spiritual meaning:

_____

_____

_____

When the "highest good" means letting go of someone or a beloved pet, embracing the higher vibration definition can be more challenging. Sometimes, it helps to acknowledge another being will be on your "team" watching over you from afar.

The beauty of the term is in turning over an outcome to a higher power. It's freeing. It removes the responsibility people sometimes take upon themselves to fix something that isn't theirs to fix. It can remove guilt.

Is it possible for a loved one who crosses the Rainbow Bridge to be as much in service, if not more, from the other side? I trust in that possibility because I've felt it. Doing so can facilitate forgiveness and make more room in your heart for higher vibrations and a stronger overall sense of well-being.

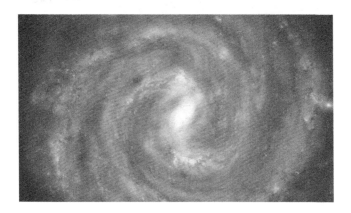

My acceptance of the "highest good" began as an intellectual exercise. Gradually, the thought process turned into an act of trust in my heart, and then the acceptance became part of my being. Respecting your higher powers' ability to guide you can become a cellular experience, transforming everything into a teaching moment. Knowing my significant lessons become opportunities to save another person time, discomfort, or pain often lightens the intensity and accelerates the process.

If you enjoy meditations, here is a link to one focusing on the highest good; enjoy, and feel free to share. https://youtu.be/3DO0rdHu3d8

What's the biggest takeaway from this chapter?

_____

_____

"Your sacred space is where you can find yourself again and again."

                 -    *Joseph Campbell*

Chapter 5

Opening Sacred Space

If sacred space is a new term for you, imagine calling forth cosmic assistance and protection to surround you, a client, or any area inside or outside with benevolent, loving energy. Within such spaces, magical things happen. You can open sacred space in any number of ways. My protocol has evolved over the years and will continue to shift as I'm directed by Spirit. Someone once asked me after a ceremony if I ever doubted the ancestors and other guides I call would come. Never, I replied. As I open space, each guide I call is vivid. I feel, see, and often hear them. You, too, can develop this skill with practice.

Here's a script to help you open your version of sacred space. Embellish as guided. Above and beyond all else, your intention for the highest good is what ensures the success of a safe, protective container for any ceremony or healing you facilitate. The first part is to request Earth Mother, and the second is for the Divine.

"Earth Mother, Sweet Mother, Pachamama, thank you for everything you provide to make this earth walk possible. Thank you for the waters that flow through and around you. Thank you for the bountiful

harvests that nourish me/us. Thank you for all you provide that shelters, supports, and protects me/us. Come, hold me gently, and nurture me/us as I/we embark on this journey of clearing/healing."

"To the Divine, the celestial beings, Creator, the ancestors, and my/our guides (list them individually if inspired), thank you for your protection and guidance. Come hold space with me/us and for me/us as I enter this journey of clearing or healing."

When you finish your session, thank Earth Mother and the Divine using a closing version of the opening prayer. Modify as you feel moved, expressing from the heart.

Many sacred items can be incorporated into the
practice of opening and closing your version of
sacred space. In section two, chapter two read
about acquiring tools.

What's the biggest takeaway from this chapter?

_____

_____

Section 2

Clearing Techniques

Best Practices

Have you ever felt the temptation to open a book and start on whatever page the universe guided you toward? I have plenty of times. If you've practiced other cleansing techniques for at least six months, you may find these practices easy to incorporate. However, the reverence for this or any other spiritual practice and the value of opening your version of sacred space cannot be stressed enough. If you are just beginning this journey, please review, at the very least, Chapter 4 on the highest good and Chapter 5 on opening sacred space before proceeding.

Holding space for the highest good as you explore these practices.

"There is no mistaking the wisdom of the body when you allow it the opportunity to guide you."

- Mountain Flower

Chapter 1

Muscle Testing

When you start performing cleansing exercises, you may wonder how you know if something is complete. Sometimes it's obvious, others not.

Chances are you won't be able to turn to someone and ask them. For this check and balance, muscle testing is my go-to tool. There are multiple ways to do it, but what I'm sharing is my favorite. I prefer it over a pendulum as those can be manipulated, whereas my body won't let me; I've tried!

In the beginning, your intellect may question the validity of your body; that's natural. If you sense movement, regardless of how subtle, please trust it until the exercise becomes second nature. Closing your eyes may help if you have good balance. Perhaps stand near a wall at first.

Doing this with eyes open works just as well; look for a focal point to avoid distractions.

Begin by standing with your feet hip-width distance apart with your arms by your side. Wearing shoes is alright, but I prefer bare feet and especially love standing in the grass or on the soil. Be on as level a surface as possible. Over time, it won't matter what surface you're standing on as your sensitivities to movement increase. You'll likely evolve to getting the same feedback while sitting. Your body becomes the pendulum in this exercise. You'll be asking a series of yes/no questions to obtain answers based on your body's intuitive knowledge with support from your higher power and Earth Mother. When your body moves forward, that's a yes; when it moves backward, it's a no. I've had NOs that almost put me on the floor. I've also been known to ask a question differently to attempt to manipulate an answer. Although I may not like an answer, I respect it unless I sense it's off. What might cause an answer to feel off?

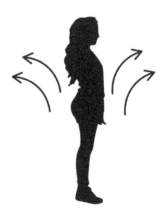

Asking questions from a low-vibrational state of panic, fear, anxiety, illness, or extreme fatigue can energetically confuse an outcome. During such states, I crave answers, but my body isn't a clear enough channel to respond accurately. Making lists of things to muscle test for when I feel more aligned helps me remember the questions and breeze through them when I'm energetically ready.

Although I may record the questions digitally on my phone, I like to write them down on paper, preferably with a pencil, before I begin testing. Using pencil and paper feels more organic, aligned, and flexible for me, but give yourself permission to do whatever feels best for you. Having some paper also supports noting any additional questions that arise or juicy information you get.

Practice makes progress. The more you practice, the more you'll trust your body, the stronger your sense of well-being, and the kinder you'll be to yourself and others. Gradually, you'll feel more empowered because the answers you used to get from others can now be sourced from within. Any apprehension about following another person's advice because it feels off, or guilt for ignoring someone's recommendations, gets eliminated.

I could write a book about all the uses for muscle testing; until then, here are my favorite ways to use it:

- Confirmation of which event I ought to facilitate at a studio when invited to do anything I like
- Confirming a hunch

- Testing food or supplements to confirm they are for my highest good
- If I don't feel like going somewhere, I'll ask if it's in my highest good to stay home

The facial expressions of folks using this technique for the first time are priceless, like a child at Disneyland. Have fun, trust your innate ability to answer yes/no questions for yourself, and get creative with new ways you can use this tool for your highest good.

What's the biggest takeaway from this chapter?

_____

_____

"When you place your order with the Universe and wait patiently, detached from the outcome, the most extraordinary things come your way!"

— Mountain Flower

Chapter 2

Acquiring Sacred Tools

From feathers to candles to crystals to smudge mix, it's fun building an array of items for different clearing and illuminating exercises.

Tempting as it is to rush to your favorite metaphysical shop or online merchant, I prefer the more energetically aligned approach of asking for guidance on what wants to assist. Asking also creates a delicious anticipation around what will come.

I've had tools gifted to me in the most fascinating ways! One such circumstance happened when I accompanied my husband to a networking event at the last minute. He introduced me to a woman who felt like a long-lost friend. After a lengthy conversation, she excused herself, stating she had to go home and get something meant to be for me - a recent acquisition from the week before that found her at a pawn shop. She began to leave the shop because the merchant was asking far more than she had in her pocket. He tried to barter. She offered him the twenty-dollar bill she had, and he accepted. These tools were the ideal complement for one of my healing protocols used with one-to-one clients. Had I not gone to this event, who knows how long it would've taken for our paths to cross?

I've also received things from friends, and sometimes, years after they find them, they wait for a sign or divine guidance about when it's time for me to have them. Most often nature provides the bounty of tools I use. Feathers are what come most frequently, sometimes gifted as the entire bird. I always respect such gifts and ask what I meant to use and how. Buying sacred items from the winged one feels forced. You could be at a powwow and drawn to a smudge fan. More power to you if that's the case; the directive could be a form of divine guidance. The purer your intent, the more will flow your way.

Realizing the beauty of such things, consider something flashy, which could be the ego demanding recognition. Simple things from nature are equally if not more effective because they find you and present themselves. There's also the intent behind the creation of such crafts and the energy of the person during the creation process to consider. When in nature and something finds you, be conscious of giving back. I love to blow a prayer of thanks into some smudge mix and sprinkle it where I found the treasure.

Once you set your intent that the universe supports your every desire in some way, you'll find things show up all the time. Feathers are a terrific example. This is another case of putting your order in and detaching from the outcome; you trust what you'd like will come while remaining detached from any specifics and then detaching from you'll get it.

Candles make a lovely addition to any ceremony. A note about purchasing candles: Consider beeswax or coconut oil products scented with the purest essential oils you can find. Better yet, consider making your own candles. Most folks don't realize that paraffin candles are fragranced with artificial ingredients and are endocrine disruptors. Sure, they smell great, but the physiological damage is worth noting. If you have these types of candles and don't want to throw them away, use them in a well-ventilated area or in the presence of an air filter. Even better, use them outside.

When lighting and extinguishing candles, do so deliberately, with intention upon lighting and a prayer of thanks when blowing out.

Lastly, please cleanse any new tool before using it. Read more about this in the next chapter.

What's the biggest takeaway from this chapter?

_____

_____

"How you do anything is how you do everything."

- Martha Beck

Chapter 3

Tool Cleansing

Any item used as a tool for cleansing will pick up some of the energy it helped remove. There are a variety of processes you can use; if unclear which one is most appropriate, go with one you really enjoy or muscle test which protocol the tool wants. You can also hold the tool to your ear and listen to which method it prefers. I prefer to cleanse tools immediately after a session or within the next 24 hours at the latest. Do what you can and be satisfied it's enough.

On the note of cleansing, I also use muscle testing to confirm that any space I work in is clean before every session or ceremony. If I get a consistent NO that a space I'm about to work in isn't clean, I begin asking questions about things in the room that may be holding a heavy vibration. You can consider muscle testing to ask if your tools are clean. If you get a NO after cleansing, you can ask if it's best to repeat the same cleansing protocol you just used or if another protocol is in order.

My favorite cleansing technique is smudging. Either use a premade mix, white sage leaves, smudge sticks, san palo, bay leaves, or anything else you're called to use, or in a pinch, use smoke from tobacco or a fire. Set your intention before beginning any cleansing protocol and open your version of sacred space. Remember to ask if the item is clean, give thanks when finished, and close sacred space. After you smudge, discard all smudge to Earth Mother with a prayer of thanks. I prefer to use loose products unless I have a lot of smudging. Many folks reuse smudge sticks; however, I don't follow this practice.

In the resource section, I'll share where you can get some of the smudge mix I've been making since 2004.

Another technique I use when in a hurry is water. If your item can withstand water (selenite crystals cannot), you can hold it under cool running water and blow into the top of the item at the same time. Set your intention that your breath and the water will perform an adequate cleansing.

Before beginning any cleansing protocol, open your version of sacred space. Remember to ask if the item is clean, give thanks when finished, and close sacred space.

When you have more time, another option is to soak an item in salt water or place it in salt and let it sit for 24 hours or longer. Remember to ask if the item is clean, give thanks when finished, and close sacred space.

You can also spray your tools with sacred water. Many products are available, but you may also want to make your own.

Another option is cleansing your tool above a candle or fire flame.

What's the biggest takeaway from this chapter?

_____

_____

"I will not let anyone walk through my mind with their dirty feet."

                         -     *Mahatma Gandhi*

Chapter 4

Basic Self-Cleansing

Before you begin clearing energy centers or places of discomfort, let's review the concept of energetically opening and closing an area.

Unwinding or opening an area to facilitate letting go of low-vibration energy requires counterclockwise movements.

This image is viewed from the back. Pretend you see the movements and copy the motions. The point of the arrow is on the right elbow, or 3 p.m. for unwinding and on the left elbow or at 9 am for rewinding.

Counterclockwise to unwind

Clockwise to rewind

Thumbs up position with right hand, see direction thumb curves

Thumbs up position with left hand, see direction thumb curves

Sealing a chakra after cleansing is done in a clockwise motion.

For working on yourself, imagine your body is the face of a clock. Your forehead is 12 o'clock, your left elbow is 3 o'clock, your feet are 6 o'clock, and your right elbow is 9 o'clock.

To unwind any energy center or area on the body, you'll begin at 12, then move your hand or tool to 9, then 6, then 3, and finish at 12. A set of three circular motions is recommended but not necessary. Make a swoosh sound, and imagine you're grabbing something with your fingertips and pulling it out of the area you're working on.

As you become more comfortable with the motions, practice exhaling as you unwind each circle. After the third circular motion, I envision all energetic traces of what I'm clearing having left my body.

Visualize energetically drawing out what you intend to heal.

The following best practices are applicable for all exercises shared in this book, regardless of clearing or illuminating, is as follows:

- Prepare your space by gathering any tools you're drawn to use
- Set a specific intention for what you're cleansing
- Cleanse your space
- Set a specific intention for healing or another outcome you want
- Trust in the process
- Open your version of sacred space

Best practices for after a session are:

- Say a prayer of thanks
- Close your version of sacred space
- Cleanse the room
- Cleanse your tools
- Journal your experience

If you're using your hands only, which I do half the time, keep the fingers closed and the palm facing the body.

A Basic Clearing Session

You can sit up or lie down for this exercise. To begin, breathe in, drawing up from the earth. Visualize a counterclockwise spiral starting at the center of the torso, unwinding the entire body energetically. On the exhale, envision all energetic particles that have loosened up, draining, dripping, and dropping into Earth Mother. See her graciously receiving. She is willing to serve and is waiting for you to ask. Repeat the full-body unwinding three times. If you still feel heaviness or discomfort of any kind, repeat the process two more times. Once the area feels lighter or clean, proceed to the next step.

On the inhale, envision a beam of white light coming through the top of the head, heart, or any other chakra that calls to you. Because of my history of trauma, the heart is usually my go-to center. On the exhale, distribute this light throughout the entire body. Repeat three times. Reiki complements this process nicely. Refer to best practices after a session.

Clearing A Specific Area of Pain or Discomfort

Follow the best practices for preparing your session.

- Prepare your space by gathering any tools you're drawn to use
- Set a specific intention for what you're cleansing
- Cleanse your space
- Set a specific intention for healing or another outcome you want
- Trust in the process
- Open your version of sacred space

Breathe in, drawing up from Earth Mother, and envision her nurturing, loving energy coming into the area of pain or discomfort. If you want to work on multiple areas, address one area at a time, working on as many areas as you made time for per session. On the exhale, envision the low vibration, the pain, inflammation, discomfort, or unease leaving the body.

On the inhale, see a beam of white light coming through the top of the head. On the exhale, distribute this light throughout the entire body and into the areas you have cleansed. Repeat three times. Reiki complements this process nicely.

Refer to best practices after a session:

- Say a prayer of thanks
- Close your version of sacred space
- Cleanse the room
- Cleanse your tools
- Journal your experience

What's the biggest takeaway from this chapter?

_____

_____

"Do not try to fix whatever comes in your life. Fix yourself in such a way that whatever comes, you will be fine."

—Sadhguru

Chapter 5

Next-level Clearing

R efer to best practices before starting a
session:

•Prepare your space by gathering any
tools you're drawn to use

• Set a specific intention for what you're
cleansing

• Cleanse your space

- Set a specific intention for healing or another outcome you want
- Trust in the process
- Open your version of sacred space

Begin by calling a specific guide or multiple guides to assist when you open space. Refer to section one, chapter three, for your list of guides if you're just beginning to work with them or are unsure which guide/guides want to help you. Pretend you see their movements and copy their motions. Breathe in, drawing up from the earth. Visualize a counterclockwise spiral starting at the center of the torso, unwinding the entire body energetically. On the exhale, use audible breath (make the swoosh sound) and envision any loosened energetic particles draining, dripping, and dropping into Earth Mother. See her graciously receiving. She is willing to serve and is waiting for you to ask. Repeat three times. If you have any sense that an area isn't fully cleansed, muscle testing helps to confirm. Ask if an area is clear. If you get a no, you can ask if it's best to repeat the type of cleansing you just used or if another protocol is in order.

On the inhale, see a beam of white light coming through the top of the head. On the exhale, distribute this light throughout the entire body. Repeat three times.

Best practices for after your session:

- Say a prayer of thanks
- Close your version of sacred space
- Cleanse the room
- Cleanse your tools
- Journal your experience
- Consider gifting something to the guide or guides who came to assist by placing food, smudge mix, or something you deem sacred out in nature

What's the biggest takeaway from this chapter?

_____

_____

"If there is magic on this planet, it is contained in water."

- *Loren Eiseley*

Chapter 6

Shower Cleansing

R efer to best practices before starting a session:

•Prepare your space by gathering any tools you're drawn to use, other than your hands; I rarely use anything besides my hands for this protocol.

- Set a specific intention for what you intend to cleanse; using the term "tune-up" or "general cleanse" is acceptable if that's what you want
- Cleanse your space; I don't always cleanse the shower, so if you are tight on time, it's okay to skip this step
- Trust in the process
- Open your version of sacred space

Review the counterclockwise and clockwise movements on your body. This image is viewed from the back; pretend you see the movements and copy the motions.

Counterclockwise to unwind

Thumbs up position with right hand, see direction thumb curves

Clockwise to rewind

Thumbs up position with left hand, see direction thumb curves

Audible breath enhances this exercise. On each exhale during the cleansing portion, pucker the lips as if blowing out a candle, making a sound like you were mimicking the wind.

Once in the shower, stand facing the showerhead and unwind each energy center beginning at the root chakra, or work exclusively on the one you're drawn to.

If one chakra feels unsettled, you can focus on that one alone. If you can make more time, I recommend clearing all seven main centers at least once a week. Daily is optimal if you are frequently in a mixed-vibration environment.

Make your unwinding motions in groups of three. Visualize each inhale as a vacuum collecting the energetic components of what you want to let go. Each exhale is removing the energy you intend to move. It may be helpful to visualize each inhale as a counterclockwise swirling within the body as your hand moves in the same counterclockwise manner. On every exhale, make a swoosh sound while imagining you're grabbing something with your fingertips and pulling it out of the center you're working on. Visualize energetically drawing out what you intend to clear.

Your combined breath and intention can move mountains; trust it is more than possible, it is probable!

Remember, when working on the back, intention is everything. Some spots are hard to reach and require your imagination to visualize the protocol's effectiveness. Trust that you're reaching the center or centers with the support of your guides and your intent.

Proceed to each chakra until you've cleared the crown. If you're having a particularly challenging time, do the entire cleansing process on your back.

After you unwind three times, muscle test and ask your body if the center is clean. If you get a NO, ask if the front needs another round or if you meant to clear the back. Proceed accordingly.

Remember, your hand or tool is an extension of divine light and incredibly powerful because you trust it to be so!

Now that you've cleared and made space, it's time to fill and seal each center. If you worked only on the front, you would not need to work on the back centers.

Start by imagining the beautiful properties of water: its uninhibited ability to flow, its ability to hold energy, and its ability to reflect light. Other things may come to you; add to the list as you feel, sense, and intuit more.

You're now moving your hands in a clockwise motion. Begin with the root chakra or the specific center you were working with. As you feel the water showering on the body, bring in the properties you envisioned into each center in rounds of three. Take an audible deep breath on the third clockwise circle and feel the center fed and full. Then, press your hand gently three times over the center to complete the sealing. Reiki complements this process nicely.

Express thanks to the water, your guides, and any tools you used. You can cleanse your tools before leaving the shower to save a step. If you choose to do so, step to the side of the water so the stream of water doesn't touch you.

You can also turn the showerhead off and blow through any tool while the water runs over it from the bathtub spout. You want anything the tool picked up to go down the drain, not back on your person. If there is no tub spout, I recommend cleaning the tools in the sink. Inhale, bringing light into the top of the head, then blow into the top of each item, envisioning the combination of your intent in this vibrationally heightened state, your breath, and the water as cleansing tools. Imagine the water carrying any residual heaviness from the tool and sending it down to Earth Mother for transforming the energy into a nurturing energy or energetic compost.

Best practices for after your session:

- Say a prayer of thanks
- Close your version of sacred space
- Cleanse the room if called
- Cleanse your tools if you used any
- Journal your experience
- Consider gifting something to the guide or guides who came to assist by placing food, smudge mix, or something you deem sacred out in nature

What's the biggest takeaway from this chapter?

_____

_____

"Let the rising heat of determination melt away obstacles."

- Unknown

Chapter 7

Candle or Fire Cleansing

Refer to best practices before starting a session:

- •Prepare your space by gathering any tools you're drawn to use
- Set a specific intention for what you're cleansing
- Cleanse your space

- Set a specific intention for healing or another outcome you want
- Trust in the process
- Open your version of sacred space

Begin by calling a specific guide or multiple guides to assist when you open space. If you are just beginning to work with them or are unsure which guide/guides want to help you, refer to section one, chapter three, for your list of guides. Envision them as though they were in front of you. Review the counterclockwise and clockwise movements on your body.

Counterclockwise to unwind

Thumbs up position with right hand, see direction thumb curves

Clockwise to rewind

Thumbs up position with left hand, see direction thumb curves

If one chakra feels unsettled, you can focus on that alone. However, I prefer to do all seven in this protocol. Do what you can make time for, and trust it's enough. Sometimes, a quick

ceremony is all that's required to take the edge off and get you through the day. Feel your way.

Make your unwinding motions in groups of three. Visualize each inhale as a vacuum collecting the energetic components of what you want to let go. Each exhale is removing the energy you intend to move. It may be helpful to visualize each inhale as a counterclockwise swirling within the body as your hand moves in the same counterclockwise manner. On every exhale, make a swoosh sound while imagining you're grabbing something with your fingertips and pulling it out of the center you're working on. Visualize energetically drawing out what you intend to clear.

The combination of your breath and your intention can move mountains; trust it is more than possible; it's probable.

Remember, when working on the back, intention is everything. Some spots are hard to reach and require your imagination to visualize the protocol's effectiveness. Trust that you're reaching the center or centers with the support of your guides and your intent. If it's helpful, envision a beam of light coming through the hand that's doing the unwinding.

Stand or sit facing the candle or fire and unwind each energy center, beginning at the root chakra. Work in groups of three. After you unwind three times, muscle test and ask your body if the center is clean. If you get a NO, ask if the front needs another round or if you ought to clean the back. Proceed accordingly. Remember, when working on the back, intention is everything. Some spots are hard to reach and require your imagination to visualize the protocol's effectiveness and trust that you're reaching them.

Now that you've cleansed and made space, it's time to fill and seal each center. If you worked only on the front, you wouldn't need to work on the back centers. Start by imagining the beautiful properties of fire—the glow, the warmth, the power, and its ability to transform matter. Be open to whatever energetically supportive guide, vision, or sensation that comes into your awareness and embrace it. The more you practice and trust your expanding awareness, the more will come through. You can also tell your guides you're ready for more.

Clockwise to rewind

Thumbs up position with left hand, see direction thumb curves

This image is viewed from the back; pretend you see the movements and copy the motions.

Move your hands clockwise to rewind each center. Begin with the root chakra, or if you're working with only one center, focus there. As you feel the warmth of the flame, move your hands in a cupping motion 24" over the fire as though you are capturing the energetic essence of the flames and bringing them into the body. Bring in the properties you envisioned into each center in rounds of three. Take an audible deep breath on the third clockwise circle and feel the center fed and full. Then, press your hand gently three times over the center to complete the sealing. Reiki complements this process nicely.

When working with candles, blow out the candle deliberately as you are finished. If this protocol resonates with you, you can either work with single-use candles and dispose of them after each use or designate a specific candle for this work. If using a fire, separate the wood, mix the ash and coals while saying a prayer of thanks, and allow it to burn out safely.

Once the fire has burned completely, put the wood and ash into the compost. I don't recommend reusing the wood. As you place the wood or ash in the compost, envision Earth Mother transforming the energy into nurturing energy or energetic compost.

Best practices for after your session:

- Say a prayer of thanks
- Close your version of sacred space
- Cleanse the room
- Cleanse your tools
- Journal your experience
- Consider gifting something to the guide or guides who came to assist by placing food, smudge mix, or something you deem sacred out in nature

What's the biggest takeaway from this chapter?

_____

_____

"Burn away what no longer serves and emerge renewed like a phoenix."

- Unknown

Chapter 8

Advanced Candle or Fire Cleansing

There is always an uplevel for cleansing exercises. When you turn self-care into an art form and make the time, you can have the most incredible experiences. When using multiple candles, I prefer to light them in a clockwise direction, and the same goes for extinguishing them. For doing heavier work, I recommend using tea lights and disposing of them afterward. If you're working indoors, try to use beeswax or coconut oil candles with natural fragrances to avoid endocrine disruption. Always ensure your candles are set on a flat, level surface.

Uplevel option 1: Perform a muscle test to determine which chakra has the lowest vibration. Then, purchase a candle of the corresponding color.

Root - red
Sacral - orange
Solar plexus - yellow
Heart - green
Throat - blue
Third eye - indigo
Crown - white

Uplevel option 2: Perform a muscle test to determine which chakra has the lowest vibration. Purchase four candles of the appropriate color to have one in each of the four directions.

Uplevel option 3: Perform a muscle test to determine which chakra has the lowest vibration. Purchase twelve candles of the appropriate color and work within the circle of candles.

Refer to best practices before starting a session:

- Prepare your space by gathering any tools you're drawn to use
- Set a specific intention for cleansing
- Cleanse your space
- Set a specific intention for healing or another outcome you want
- Trust in the process
- Open your version of sacred space

Call a specific guide or multiple guides to assist when you open space. Refer to section one, chapter three, for your list of guides if you're just beginning to work with them or are unsure which guide/guides want to help you. Envision them as though they were in front of you. If one chakra feels unsettled, you can focus on that alone. However, I prefer to do all seven centers in this protocol.

For reference, the diagrams for unwinding and rewinding each chakra are noted.

Counterclockwise to unwind

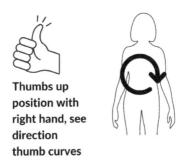

Thumbs up position with right hand, see direction thumb curves

This image is viewed from the back; pretend you see the movements and copy the motions.

Make your unwinding motions in groups of three. Visualize each inhale as a vacuum collecting the energetic components of what you want to let go. Each exhale is removing the energy you intend to move. It may be helpful to visualize each inhale as a counterclockwise swirling within the body as your hand moves in the same counterclockwise manner. On every exhale, make a swoosh sound while imagining you're grabbing something with your fingertips and pulling it out of the center you're working on. Visualize energetically drawing out what you intend to clear. After you unwind three times, muscle test and ask your body if the center is clean. If you get a NO, ask if the front needs another round or if you ought to clean the back. Proceed accordingly. Remember, when working on the back, intention is everything. Some spots are hard to reach and require your imagination to visualize the protocol's effectiveness and trust that you're reaching them.

Now that you've cleansed and made space, it's time to fill and seal each center. If you worked only on the front, you would not need to work on the back centers. Start by imagining the beautiful properties of fire—the beautiful glow, the warmth, the power, and its ability to transform matter. You can make a list in advance of what fire represents for you or go with what surfaces in the moment. Other things may come to you; add to the list as you feel, sense, and intuit more.

Begin with the root chakra, or if you're working with only one center, focus there. As you feel the warmth of the flame, move your hands in a cupping motion 24" over the fire as though you are capturing the energetic essence of the flames and bringing them into the body. Proceed with caution; stay high enough above the flames to remain safe. Trust that you're capturing the flames' essence at whatever height you are above them.

Clockwise to rewind

Thumbs up position with left hand, see direction thumb curves

This image is viewed from the back; pretend you see the movements and copy the motions.

Bring the properties you envisioned into each center in rounds of three. Take an audible deep breath on the third clockwise circle and feel the center fed and full. Then, press your hand gently three times over the center to complete the sealing. Sometimes, I linger here because the warmth of the flames fills my being, and I want to stay in the energy longer. Reiki complements this process nicely.

If using a candle, blow it out deliberately. If this protocol resonates with you, you can either work with single-use candles and dispose of them after each use or designate a specific candle for this work. If using a fire, separate the wood, mix the ash and coals while saying a prayer of thanks, and allow it to burn out safely.

Once the fire has burned completely, put the wood and ash into the compost. I don't recommend reusing the wood. As you place the wood or ash in the compost, envision Earth Mother transforming the energy into nurturing energy or energetic compost.

Best practices for after your session:

- Say a prayer of thanks
- Close your version of sacred space
- Cleanse the room
- Cleanse your tools
- Journal your experience
- Consider gifting something to the guide or guides who came to assist by placing food, smudge mix, or something you deem sacred out in nature

What's the biggest takeaway from this chapter?

_____

_____

"The people who trigger us to feel negative emotion are messengers. They are messengers for the unhealed parts of our being."

- Teal Swan

Chapter 9

Quick Clearing Away From Home

Sometimes, you can get caught off guard and need help quickly to get through the rest of the day. This practice is intended to serve as a tool in an urgent, energetically draining situation. Consider practicing this with someone a few times so you feel more comfortable when you must use it. Explain to them you are building a skill and want their help. Ensure it's someone you trust and who is open to energy work. Follow best practices for opening and closing sacred space for these skill-building sessions.

- Prepare your space by gathering any tools you're drawn to use
- Set a specific intention
- Cleanse your space
- Set a specific intention for healing or another outcome you want
- Trust in the process
- Open your version of sacred space

When you practice, you want to invoke a low-vibration energy to emit from your helper and beam towards you. One way is to ask the person with you to think of the last thing that bothered them. Ask them to focus that lower vibration energy on you when they are clear. If they are thinking about rainbows and puppies, they are not helping. Offer to smudge them afterward if they have trouble shaking off the memory.

Reassure them this is an exercise for your highest good.

You're setting multiple intentions here: first, for what you want to clear; second, that this exercise is effective; and third, that your imagination will move energy however you want it to move.

Let's presume you've practiced and want to implement this away from home. Best practices for opening sacred space might be as simple as:

- Set a specific intention for healing or protection or both
- Trust in the process
- Open your version of sacred space

Remember the power of your intent. I've been known to open sacred space when I'm in a hurry by placing my palm in each of the six directions as a quick wave. I trust the ancestors and guides will come and support me. For whatever reason this happens, I always remember my reverence for this work.

If you can find a room, a closet, a place where you'll be undisturbed, fantastic, but that isn't always the case. The restroom can be a great place. For such times when you cannot escape to a cubicle or another room and are stuck in a meeting, imagine that the simple caress on the top of your hand in a counterclockwise manner will cleanse whatever you want relief from. You can do a deeper cleansing at home. This exercise is intended for urgent situations.

Before you begin, imagine a white light coming in through the top of your hand, extending down your neck and arm, and coming out the palm of your hand. Consider this your lightsaber. **Trust this will happen on command.**

For specific areas of discomfort, imagine the body in two halves. When you rub the top of your left or right hand, you cleanse a left or right foot, knee, shoulder, etc. If your discomfort is energetic and expansiv/ throughout, pick either hand and use it to represent the entire body.

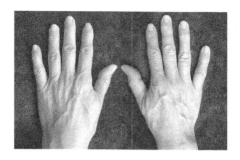

As you look at the top of your hand, the middle finger serves as 12 o'clock, and the wrist is 6 p.m., 3, and 6 o'clock, depending on which hand you're working with. You can also use the palm if you have to have your hand under a desk; if so, imagine the clock on your palm with 9 o'clock on the thumb or pinky, depending on which hand you're using.

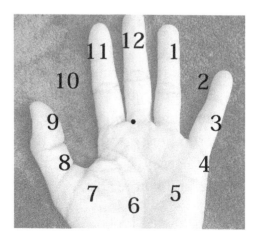

See the hand you're using to clear as a lightsaber, an incredible tool. Then, envision the top or palm of your hand as the specific point that feels afflicted or the top of the hand as the entire half of the body. After each caress (you can do one counterclockwise circle or three), flick your fingers like you're shooing away a fly or removing water droplets from your fingers.

After the unwinding, you'll fill and seal the area with white light by rubbing the hand in a clockwise manner, envisioning the light moving through the entire body and radiating to create a cocoon of light around you. Inhale white light through the top of your head and, on the exhale, imagine you've empowered a forcefield of protective light around you. This light emanates through your breath, through your cells, and throughout your energy field. If another color light comes in, great, use it. Remember to press gently three times with either your fingertips or the palm of your hand. Add Reiki if you're able.

Set another intention: the exercise will protect you until you get home. Ask for your higher power to help you hold this protective light. You can also call on any spiritual or animal guides, ancestors, or other deities with whom you have a relationship.

Best practices for after your session:

- Say a prayer of thanks
- Close your version of sacred space

What's the biggest takeaway from this chapter?

_____

_____

"To the flame that ignites my smudge, to the sage that clears my heaviness, I thank the smoke for taking my prayers to Great Spirit and Earth Mother for providing these sacred tools."

- Mountain Flower

Chapter 10

Smudge Work

If you've ever been to one of my events, you know how much I love to smudge. This technique can be done anytime you feel something heavy. It's best done outside. I use this exercise whenever I come home from an event in case I unintentionally pick up anything.

Ingredients needed:

- White sage or sage from your garden, smudge mix, palo santo, or bay leaves in a pinch
- If burning loose material, a shell is helpful to hold the smudge mix
- A lighter
- A feather or wing if you have one, but if not, your hand is sufficient

Refer to best practices before starting a session:

- Prepare your space by gathering the tools you're drawn to use
- Set a specific intention for cleansing
- I don't cleanse outside spaces when I smudge
- Trust in the process
- Open your version of sacred space

Call a specific guide or multiple guides to assist when you open space. Refer to section one, chapter three, for your list of guides if you're beginning to work with them or are unsure which guide/guides want to help you.

Review winding and unwinding motions. This image is viewed from the back; pretend you see the movements and copy the motions.

Counterclockwise to unwind

Thumbs up
position with
right hand, see
direction
thumb curves

Clockwise to rewind

Thumbs up
position with
left hand, see
direction
thumb curves

Hold the burning sage or other sacred product in front of the root chakra with one hand. Sometimes, the shells can get hot, so please use caution. You can double up the shells, attach the shell to a piece of wood, or use a potholder. You'll use your other hand or a feather as a lightsaber. Unwind the chakra in rounds of three.

If one chakra feels unsettled, you can focus on that alone. However, I prefer to do all seven in this protocol. Do what you can and trust it's enough unless your body tells you otherwise.

Make your unwinding motions in groups of three. Visualize each inhale as a vacuum collecting the energetic components of what you want to let go. The smoke empowers each exhale to remove the energy you intend to move. It may be helpful to visualize each inhale as a counterclockwise swirling within the body as your hand or tool moves in the same counterclockwise manner. If using your hands on every exhale, make a swoosh sound while imagining you're grabbing something with your fingertips and pulling it out of the center you're working on. Visualize energetically drawing out what you intend to clear.

After you unwind three times, muscle test and ask your body if the center is clean. If you get a NO, ask if the front needs another round or if you ought to clean the back. Proceed accordingly. Remember, when working on the back, intention is everything. Some spots are hard to reach and require your imagination to visualize the protocol's effectiveness and trust that you're reaching them.

Proceed to each chakra until you've cleared the crown. I usually do the bottom of my feet after the crown, but you can do the feet first. If you're having a particularly challenging time, repeat the entire cleansing process on the back. Remember, when working on the back, intention is everything. Some spots are hard to reach and require your imagination to visualize the protocol's effectiveness and trust that you're reaching them.

After ceremonies, I'm usually filled and overflowing, and I do not feel a pressing need to feed my centers. I cleanse to help eliminate any residual energies that may have hitched a ride. Muscle test to ask if your chakras want to be fed or if they feel complete.

If you are called to fill and seal each center, you can do the following:

While placing your hands over each center, inhale light through the top of your head and envision it moving down to each center, either through the body and out of your hands or from the head down the spinal column. Feel the light, heat, or tingling sensations through your palms. You can do reiki. You can call your angels or spiritual guides to feed each center. You can feed love with your intention.

In daylight, you can lay in the grass and feed each center with the sun. If it's at night, you can feed each center with starlight or cosmos energy

When filling the centers, if you worked on the front only, you would not need to work on the back centers unless you felt called to do so.

Once finished, put the burned smudge or other sacred item into the compost. I don't recommend reusing any leftover smudge. As you place the ashes in the compost, envision Earth Mother transforming the energy into a nurturing energy or energetic compost.

Best practices for after your session:

- Say a prayer of thanks
- Close your version of sacred space
- Cleanse your tools; you can use the smudge before extinguishing it. I also

      like to leave the shell outside on the ground to let Earth Mother cleanse it

- Journal your experience
- Consider gifting something to the guide or guides who came to assist by placing food, smudge mix, or something you deem sacred out in nature

If you're looking for a smudge made with integrity and infused with healing prayers, check out Sacred Scents. It's a mix I began making in 2004. Available on my website www.MTflower.com/offerings

What's the biggest takeaway from this chapter?

_____

_____

"When you do nothing, you feel overwhelmed and powerless. But when you get involved, you feel the sense of hope and accomplishment that comes from knowing you are working to make things better."

- Pauline R. Kezer

Chapter 11

Conscious Elimination

This protocol is the easiest to incorporate into your daily practice. Most people giggle when I talk about it, but it's extremely effective. Every time you have to eliminate, why not make it an energetic experience for the highest good?

If you want to open sacred space beforehand, you can, but I usually don't. My intention is enough. Envision that each time you eliminate, the excretion also energetically cleanses you. Drinking lots of water is helpful in stressful situations because it gives you more opportunities to cleanse.

Intention and breath can increase the effectiveness of this exercise. As in other cleansing methods, as you inhale, envision your breath collecting all the energetic debris ready to leave the body. Exhale as the body eliminates visualizing what you're letting go easily flowing from the body. Smile as you flush, and thank Spirit for sending the waste to be processed. You can also envision a counterclockwise spiral at one or all of the chakras before and as you eliminate. When finished, place your hand on each center or on the heart alone, envisioning you're filling each center with love.

Thank your higher power for remembering this technique and move on with your day feeling refreshed.

Food for thought: the next time you have digestive issues, be thankful for your body's functionality to clear out anything unhealthy!

What's the biggest takeaway from this chapter?

_____

_____

"When I'm out in the garden, my worries and anxieties seem to melt away. There's something about getting my hands dirty, feeling the rhythm of the seasons, that has a deeply cleansing effect on my spirit."

- Rosemary Gladstar

Chapter 12

Garden Cleansing

Getting in touch with Earth Mother is always healing. Contact with her is an essential part of my daily practice. My moments of tension are farther apart nowadays, but this has always served me well when I was so wound up I couldn't see straight. I'd envision weeding as an energetic cleansing exercise. Every weed I yank is either resistance I'm aware of getting pulled, or when I'm too frazzled to be that conscious of what I'm doing, I trust that each weed represents something that no longer serves and is time for it to go.

In a perfect world, you'd be letting go with love, but sometimes, that's too much to envision when you are so filled with low-vibrational energy that you're ready to explode. Consider the exercise an act of self-love.

You can also visualize pruning as a form of cleansing. Not only are you serving the plant or tree, but you're using the experience as an act of self-care with intention.

When you are finished gardening, say a prayer of thanks for Earth Mother's support and consider gifting her something.

What's the biggest takeaway from this chapter?

_____

_____

"Believe in your infinite potential. Your only limitations are those you set upon yourself."

- Roy T. Bennett

Chapter 13

How Far Can You Take Cleansing?

As far as your imagination or intuition is willing to play. From washing dishes to polishing furniture or silver, your intent is your most powerful tool! The more you practice "downloading" or following your intuitive nudges, the more will come to you and the more fun you'll have.

Everyone has their own preferred practices. Just because what I've written here works for me doesn't imply that all these practices will make their way into your routine. Use the suggestions in this book as a launching point to build confidence in your ability to clear and heal on your own. Get playful. Get creative.

If you encounter something particularly heavy, remember help is just a few clicks away. If you want a remote session or want to travel to southeastern Connecticut, let's have a conversation. I'm happy to be of service.

When you download a new practice, consider keeping it to yourself until you are comfortable with it. Negative feedback disguised as concern or help from someone could reduce your confidence if you're still learning to trust what you're doing. Everything is a process. Practice regularly. Keep asking your higher power for assistance and guidance.

When you're interested in a one-to-one session, I can be reached via email at Hello@MTflower.com or schedule a call at https://calendly.com/mtflower/connection-call

What's the biggest takeaway from this chapter?

_____

_____

–

Section 3

Illumination Exercises

"When we are grounded, we feel a deep sense of belonging and rootedness. We are anchored in the present moment, able to respond to life with clarity, wisdom, and equanimity."

- Heather Askinosie

Chapter 1

Grounding

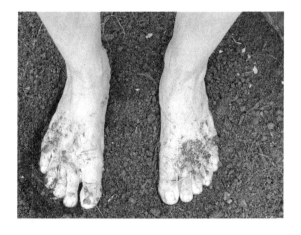

The following vibration-raising exercises can easily put you in a euphoric state. After any of these practices, give yourself some time to ease back into your body and move on with your day. Please avoid driving or using machinery immediately afterward; if you can wait at least 30 minutes to ensure your safety, that'd be ideal.

Returning to your physical body with ease helps these methods integrate and stay longer. Getting your feet in the grass is ideal if you have a backyard. Honor the beauty of your experience and make it last as long as possible.

Immediately after finishing any version of these illumination exercises, I like to stretch my arms in front of my body or lift them over my head. Extend the palms and fingers wide. Gently roll the head from side to side.

Then, stretch the legs. Extend the toes and move the feet from side to side. Tighten and release the glutes. Roll onto one side and take a few breaths. Sit up slowly. A nice touch is to hold your cheek and use your hand to raise the head, reducing pressure and tension on the neck. Give your body time to acclimate to the higher vibration. Drink lots of water. You have moved some energy and want to give anything that no longer serves you an opportunity to leave the body. The more water consumed, the more opportunities to cleanse.

Here's another thing to consider. This protocol is a common practice at the end of my ceremonies to help people remember the vibration of their experience long after it happened: Find any small item you deem sacred to serve as a token. It can be a pendant, a crystal, a stone, or anything else you want.

When you return to your body after any given illumination technique, inhale deeply to collect the energy of all the beauty, love, light, and energy flowing within. Then, with a deliberate, audible breath, blow as many times as needed to feel complete into your token. Blowing with an audible breath feels more deliberate, purposeful, and intentional.

Keep your token someplace sacred. It could be an altar, on a windowsill, or in a jewelry box. Each time you see the token, imagine your heart filling with light as it taps energetically into all the experiences it holds. Then, on days when protocol dictates you show up (work, appointments, etc.) and you aren't feeling like it, bring the token with you. It can serve as the adult version of a security blanket. You can have the token in your pocket, bra cup, or socks,

and it will empower you by emanating the love
and light you've fed it.

What's the biggest takeaway from this chapter?

_____

_____

"Each of our chakras is like a garden, requiring nourishment and care to bloom in vibrant health. When we consciously feed our chakras, we cultivate balance, harmony, and a deep sense of wholeness."

- Anodea Judith

Chapter 2

Feeding Your Energy Centers

J ust in case you opened to this chapter first, please review the grounding chapter in the beginning of this section before proceeding. When lying down, this is a great exercise but can also be done in a seated position. In addition to this protocol, I usually incorporate the following techniques into my morning routine, followed by a grounding session in the backyard.

Refer to best practices before starting a session:

- Prepare your space
- If you do this on waking, your intent for preparing and cleansing the space from bed is enough
- Set a specific intention
- Trust in the process
- Open your version of sacred space

To begin, call a specific guide or multiple guides to assist when you open space. If you're beginning to work with them or are unsure which guide/guides want to help you, refer to section one, chapter three, for your list of guides. Envision them as though they were in front of you. Review the counterclockwise and clockwise movements on your body.

Counterclockwise to unwind   **Clockwise to rewind**

Thumbs up
position with
right hand, see
direction
thumb curves

Thumbs up
position with
left hand, see
direction
thumb curves

Here is a review of the colors for each of the seven basic body chakras:

Root - red
Sacral - orange
Solar - yellow
Heart - green
Throat - blue
Third eye - indigo
Crown – white

If you're drawn to different colors, go with what you see or intuit. Your guides may have another plan for you during your experience. Each session will feel different, so be open to effectiveness regardless of who comes to help and how varied each experience feels. My practices are always shifting; no two are exactly alike. Part of the changes are my openness to what my higher self wants or brings in, what my guides suggest, and what feels aligned. My only constant is my intent for the highest good, and trusting the process becomes more beautiful than the day before.

Begin by connecting to Earth Mother with your breath. With each inhale, see/feel/sense her energy coming up into all seven energy centers simultaneously, as if you were pulling up a blanket. Is there a particular color you associate with Earth Mother? What does her energy feel like? What does it look like? Be willing to expand beyond what you are accustomed to associating.

Each inhale brings up the cyclical energy of nature that recognizes the seasonality of something you're carrying and enhances the body's ability to let it go. If you can imagine the root of a dandelion that needs two pulls to come out, your inhale represents the loosening of the soil, and your exhale is the pulling of the root.

On the exhale, imagine Earth Mother graciously receiving what your body lets go of; she takes the heaviness with open arms to process and transform into light.

Now that each center is open, the next phase brings light into each center. On the inhale, envision bringing Divine light into each center the same way, all centers simultaneously, like you're pulling a blanket down from the cosmos.

There are variations on what to do with your exhale: play with each or do what calls to you.

Phase 1: On the exhale, envision the light distributing from all chakras throughout the body. Stop here or add the next phase.

Phase 2: On the exhale, envision the light emanating from your pores filling the room. Stop here or add the next phase.

Phase 3: On the exhale, also envision each chakra illuminated by color. See an oscillating or clockwise rotating orb in each center. Begin at the root and move upward. Once you envision the crown, envision all centers with all seven colors vibrating simultaneously. Stay in this exquisite vibration for at least three breaths. Linger as long as you can.

On a day when you feel particularly charged and want to share your light with anyone or anything in a larger geographic area, on your exhale, envision the light emanating from you throughout your home and beyond to include as far as you are willing to imagine. Always send this light for the highest good attachment-free to any specific outcome.

Say prayers of thanks, close sacred space, and journal if called.

What's the biggest takeaway from this chapter?

_____

_____

"When your energy vibrates at a frequency that is within direct alignment to what the Univers has been attempting to deliver your entire life, you begin to live in the flow, and true miracles start to happen."

- Panache Desai

Chapter 3

Basic Illumination Work

J ust in case you opened to this chapter first, please review the grounding chapter before proceeding. When lying down, this is a great exercise but can also be done in a seated position. I usually incorporate all the techniques shared here into my morning routine, followed by a grounding session in the backyard.

Refer to best practices before starting a session:

- Prepare your space by gathering any tools you're drawn to use
- If you do this on waking, your intent for preparing and cleansing the space is enough
- Set a specific intention
- Cleanse your space
- Trust in the process
- Open your version of sacred space

Envision a clockwise rotating vortex of light in the color of your choice, spinning at the bottom of the feet, at the ankles, at the knees, at the hips, at each of the twenty-four vertebrae in the spine, at the elbows, at the wrists, at all the joints in the hands, at the ears, at the eyes, or anywhere else your body draws your attention. To save time on the hands and feet, I spin the vortexes on all the first knuckles, then all the second, and then where the fingers or toes come to the hand or the foot. If you can make the time to do each knuckle individually, that would be fantastic, but this process is equally effective.

Use this technique of a clockwise spiraling light with areas of pain or discomfort after a clearing exercise to accelerate healing.

Play with different colors in different areas and at different times. As your vibration shifts, trust that each exercise is for the highest good and will always result in a terrific outcome. If you plan ahead, you can use this after any of the clearing techniques.

What's the biggest takeaway from this chapter?

_____

_____

"You cannot discover new oceans unless you have the courage to lose sight of the shore."

- Andre Gide

Chapter 4

Advanced Vibration Raising

J ust in case you opened to this chapter first, please review the grounding chapter before proceeding. Although some portions are similar to the prior exercises, this protocol invites you to explore illumination even more expansively.

This is a fantastic exercise when you wake up too early because it can elevate your energy for the entire day. It has become an integral part of my morning practice.

Refer to best practices before starting a session:

- Prepare your space by gathering any tools you're drawn to use
- If you do this on waking, your intent for preparing and cleansing the space is enough
- Set a specific intention
- Cleanse your space
- Trust in the process
- Open your version of sacred space

Inhale a beautiful white or iridescent light through the top of the head or heart while simultaneously visualizing clockwise spiraling energy on the soles of both feet, then both ankles, then both knees, then both hips, then the torso, then both shoulders, then both elbows, then both wrists, then the neck, and lastly, the head.

You can play with the number of breaths you take in each area; I like a minimum of three, but when you set your intention, whatever you make time for is effective.

For the next round of breath and intention, visualize the energy moving around you to weave an energetic cocoon. Begin with the feet, then calves, then legs, hips, then the torso, including the arms and hands, and lastly, the head. Use your breath to guide how far up the body you get. I prefer to wrap the legs and arms individually and simultaneously, but do what works for you.

Inhale light into the top of the head, and on the exhale, visualize the spiraling until your lungs are empty. Inhale again and begin where you left off on the exhale. You might encompass the entire body in as few as three breaths. The goal is to surround the body while comfortably breathing. You may sense that some areas want more exhalation than others. Feel your way through it; this is an illuminating, relaxing exercise that's most effective if you take your time.

For the last round, hold the vision of your body surrounded by the beautiful cocoon of light; perhaps you can see the spiraling movement of energy without directly focusing on it. As long as you sense the energy, vibrating, spiraling, or simply glowing, it's all equally effective. On the inhale, you'll bring the light in again. Then, you'll create an additional energy sphere encompassing the cocoon you've just created. Now, you have two light layers around you, illuminating your physical and energetic body.

Bask in this energy for as long as you like; trusting Spirit will hold this for you as long as you direct it. Then, I state the following mantra before I thank the Spirit and my guides: *"I am the environment instead of a product of it."* This is especially helpful for empaths because the energy of others can be overwhelming. Repeat three times.

I love how I feel after doing this. Each time, I tap into the highest vibration my body can hold.

As my cells get accustomed, they retain the energy longer. Different guides come in with messages. Low vibrations anywhere in my vicinity become less noticeable and less impactful to my state of being.

The more you practice this protocol, the more tuned you will be to your higher power and spiritual guides. You will begin to trust any variation that comes to you. The only hard, fast rule is your intention for the highest good.

Here's to your energy field holding all the protection you'll ever need! You have much work to do in this lifetime, and Spirit wants you to be as healthy and vibrant as possible.

Many blessings through the journey of illumination.

"At any moment, you have a choice that either leads you closer to your spirit or further away from it."

-    *Thich Nhat Hanh*

Chapter 5

Take It Further

If you are interested in recordings of this material, each protocol is available for purchase. You'll find the details on my website www.MTflower.com

Wherever you are in the world, I invite you to place an order with Spirit and let them know you are open and willing to attract other like-minded people who can support you through the exploration of this work.

For every lightworker out there who is at peace taking deep dives into spiritual development, there are millions who lack the community to ask questions, guide them on where to begin, and support them along the way.

Your task on this earth walk is to live in the highest vibration possible and pay it forward. Raising your energy involves shedding what weighs you down. The best place to start is with your thoughts. Simple shifts in language do wonders for the subconscious. Consider changing the negative language to positive. The most common examples of low-vibration thoughts and language with their higher vibration counterparts are:

"I don't know how" to "I'm experimenting" or "I can't" to "I'm learning." Appreciate you are a divine creation in perpetual transformation.

The more advanced your skills become, you'll likely need more rest to allow your physical body to acclimate to the higher vibrations you are calling in.

When you venture into intense emotional practices, be gentle with yourself. Your physical body needs time to recover.

When I was thirty-five years old, my eyes began opening to the possibility that I deserved happiness and that I was worthy of anything my heart desired. It took time to get used to the idea before I began taking action. When I let Spirit know I was ready, the floodgates opened. I'm not shy about asking for a reprieve when too much comes at once, my *former* pattern was to take on three big things at once. I had so much to let go of and move into; it was the only way to get to the next phase in a timely manner. I often joke that I didn't read the fine print when Spirit handed me the contract to serve.

Trusting in the highest good and getting help when I needed it has saved me. It'd be an honor to hold space with you and for you, either in person or virtually. You're here to do spectacular things! Holding space for grounded expansion in service to what fills your heart and feeds your soul.

Knowledge is power. Information is liberating. Education is the premise of progress in every society, in every family.

Kofi Anna

Chapter 6

Chapter Summaries

T o save you flipping pages with your biggest takeaways from each chapter, use this section if you find it helpful.

Section 1 Setting the Foundation

Chapter 1 Imagination Versus Downloads

What's the biggest takeaway from this chapter?

_____

_____

Chapter 2 Trust And Truth

What's the biggest takeaway from this chapter?

_____

_____

Chapter 3 Working With Your Higher Power

What's the biggest takeaway from this chapter?

_____

_____

Chapter 4 Highest Good

What's the biggest takeaway from this chapter?

_____

_____

Chapter 5 Opening Sacred Space

What's the biggest takeaway from this chapter?

_____

_____

Section 2 Cleansing and Clearing Techniques

Chapter 1 Muscle Testing

What's the biggest takeaway from this chapter?

_____

_____

Chapter 2 Acquiring Sacred Tools

What's the biggest takeaway from this chapter?

_____

_____

Chapter 3 Tool Cleansing

What's the biggest takeaway from this chapter?

_____

_____

Chapter 4 Basic Clearing

What's the biggest takeaway from this chapter?

_____

_____

Chapter 5 Next-level Clearing

What's the biggest takeaway from this chapter?

_____

_____

Chapter 6 Shower Cleansing

What's the biggest takeaway from this chapter?

_____

_____

Chapter 7 Candle or Fire Cleansing

What's the biggest takeaway from this chapter?

_____

_____

Chapter 8 Advanced Candle or Fire Work

What's the biggest takeaway from this chapter?

_____

_____

Chapter 9 Quick Clearing Away From Home

What's the biggest takeaway from this chapter?

_____

_____

Chapter 10 Smudge Work

What's the biggest takeaway from this chapter?

_____

_____

Chapter 11 Conscious Elimination

What's the biggest takeaway from this chapter?

_____

_____

Chapter 12 Garden Cleansing

What's the biggest takeaway from this chapter?

_____

_____

Chapter 13 How Far Can You Take Cleansing?

What's the biggest takeaway from this chapter?

_____

_____

Section 3 Illumination Techniques

Chapter 1 Grounding

What's the biggest takeaway from this chapter?

_____

_____

Chapter 2 Feeding Your Energy Centers

What's the biggest takeaway from this chapter?

_____

_____

Chapter 3 Basic Illumination Work

What's the biggest takeaway from this chapter?

_____

_____

Chapter 4 Advanced Vibration Raising

What's the biggest takeaway from this chapter?

_____

_____

Chapter 5 How To Take This Work Further

What's the biggest takeaway from this chapter?

_____

_____

"We can never obtain peace in the outer world until we make peace with ourselves."

- Dalai Lama

About The Author

Mountain Flower's mission is to help people heal all sense of disconnection so they can live in alignment with their body, spirit, Earth Mother, and the Divine. Part of living in alignment is trusting and strengthening your skills to inspire others and keep paying it forward.

After decades of struggling with feeling unworthy and fully embracing her gifts, she realized that hiding and playing small took a physical toll on her body as well as the emotional, mental, and spiritual toll on her energy. In almost every healer's journey, a time comes when the pain of doing nothing is greater than the discomfort of taking action. Once she surrendered to her calling, magical things unfolded. Following her intuition and embracing the whispers from Spirit reinforce her trust in following whatever direction she gets.

A multifaceted Native American medicine woman, Mountain Flower facilitates dozens of ceremonies directed by Source. A master of holding sacred space and calling in the ancestors to support her and her clients, she has fed the hearts and souls of thousands since 1999. She is also a Karuna Reiki Master/Teacher, a six-time author at this publication, and 225-hour CYT in Forrest Yoga. Beyond North America, her influence has reached China, Nepal, and Bangladesh.

Recently embracing her lineage as a fourth-generation drum maker, Mountain Flower now makes Native American drums. Each sacred instrument is crafted in a ceremonial space and infused with her intentions for healing throughout the entire process. She also facilitates hand drum-making workshops and takes orders for hand drums made for specific intentions. For information on ordering, check her website.

If you've ever experienced the Immersion Drum Healing workshop, you know the significance of drums made with pure intent for the highest good and the power of sitting with her in sacred space. From yoga studios in CT and RI, yoga festivals, and private events, her ceremonies open hearts and souls.

People who have worked with Mountain Flower refer to her protocols as:

- *"Extremely innovative"*
- *"Deep energy work"*
- *"Life-changing"*
- *"Freeing"*

Some of the other ceremonies Mountain Flower facilitates are:

- Vibration of Wholeness
- Shamanic Journeying
- Exploring Past Lives
- Intuitive Healer
- Energetic Origin of Struggle
- Forgive Nest
- Intuitive Discussion Circle
- Energetics 101
- Ancestral Healing
- Smudging Intensive
- Fire ceremonies
- Living A Spiritual Life
- Detaching From Outcome
- Divinely Aligned

For more information about any of these ceremonies, informative articles, drumming meditations, and more, check her website: www.MTflower.com.

Follow her on Instagram or Facebook at HealingThroughYourStory

MOUNTAIN FLOWER
MEDICINE WOMAN

Other books published under her colonial name, Leslie Karen Hammond:

Conversational Intelligence is a practical guide to understanding the dynamics of effective communication.

How different would your life be if people understood you and you were clear about what you heard? Misunderstandings provide extraordinary teaching moments.

This book offers tools to discover what's behind the way you communicate to understand better why everyone else shows up in the world the way they do. Once you see how your stories and experience shape you, everyone else will begin to make more sense.

Holding Space describes Leslie's observations and experiences during the eight months she volunteered in Asia between September 2017 through February 2019. Leslie spent time with college-age women in China, Nepal, and Bangladesh who found the courage to join the World Academy for the Future of Women, a global leadership training organization.

The striking similarities found across cultural divides were remarkable. She saw parts of herself in earlier years before her clarity of purpose. Women's willingness to open their hearts reinforced the mission Leslie's devoted herself to over the last twenty years; empowering women to find their voice and use it. Expect to dive into the psyche of not just women but also paradigms of the human condition.

KEEP IT REAL

WHY WE'RE AFRAID TO SPEAK UP AND WHAT TO DO ABOUT IT

LESLIE KAREN HAMMOND

Keep It Real will help you gain a profound sense of self, achieve clarity on how you process information and awaken your compassion for others. When you are ready to start speaking your truth, it will provide tools to prepare you for the conversation.

Once you see how lifelong communication patterns are formed, you'll be better equipped to tune into what people are saying versus what they truly mean. This profound perspective on the human condition will impact how you communicate in personal and professional circles. This book will support you in feeling worthy of being heard. In the process, everyone you interact with will feel appreciated and better understood.

Women Rising is an invitation to see your journey up until this moment in a new light. You are capable of embracing your past and recognizing it as the foundation of who you are today. You are solid, strong and timeless. Every story has the ability to empower or deflate you. When you transform each life event into a teaching moment, you release the attachment to the past and make room for the future. Are you ready to give yourself permission to thrive and step into all you're capable of? A must read for all women and highly recommended for the men who support them! Leslie has been helping women find their voice and use it for over 16 years. These pages contain many of the tools she uses. The slightest shift in perspective can make a world of difference and break the cycle of unworthiness and silent suffering.

MOUNTAIN FLOWER
MEDICINE WOMAN

Deeply connective spiritual experiences

Ceremonies in studios and private functions

Drums, smudge mix, and other sacred items

Drum making workshops

One-to-one and private group sessions

Reiki certification classes

Shamanic Manifesting program

Mentoring

Customized meditations

Space cleansing

Rites of Passage

Made in the USA
Middletown, DE
07 September 2024

59880713R00117